The ABCs
of Portland's
Alphabet and Pearl Districts
(Revised Edition)

Harvey Kline

Alphabet & Pearl Publishing
PORTLAND, OREGON

Production	Jeanne Galick
Book design	Tom Sumner
Cover and maps	Karen Phillips (phillipscovers.com)
Original photography	Harvey Kline

Printed in the U.S.A.

Alphabet & Pearl Publishing
https://alphabetandpearl.wordpress.com

ISBN 978-0-692-10071-4

CONTENTS

PREFACE

WHEN MY WIFE AND I moved to Northwest Portland several years ago, besides falling in love with the city pretty much overnight, we were pleased to find the streets, south to north, listed in alphabetical order. It's good for new people and tourists. And one of the first things we learned about the street where we lived was that it bore the name of the "founder" of Portland. Moreover, historians portrayed him as a man of some mystery, about whom not much was known. Soon after that we heard the oft-repeated story of the coin toss which named the young town. I wondered if others whose names appeared on the streets of the Alphabet and Pearl Districts would yield equally interesting tales. Scholars have mined much information about this neighborhood from the days of the pioneers. It is not my intention to add to the body of original research on the subject. But it is my hope that, once in a while, readers will look up at the street signs and remember some of the people whose names they honor.

ACKNOWLEDGMENTS

I discovered quickly that one cannot write even a short book like this without incurring a lot of debts. The list is long and begins with my wife Yuko. Without her patience and technical assistance this effort would never have seen the light of day. She spent many hours, snatched from a busy work schedule, answering questions and working with me through these pages.

For this revised edition, I'm indebted to Ted Kaye, Portland history enthusiast formerly with the Oregon Historical Society. His encouragement at all stages of this book and his review of the text for historical accuracy and stylistic clarity have been invaluable.

I am grateful to Jeanne Galick for serving as production editor for this edition. Jeanne has made invaluable suggestions along the way and has worked under constantly shifting deadlines and changes in the text.

From the beginning it was Tom Sumner of Franklin, Beedle, who provided me with the production expertise necessary to pursue this project to conclusion. Tom has continued to offer his professional assistance for this edition, most especially in preparing the book for the printer. Among his many contributions, Tom designed the first edition's interior layout.

My sister Helen has given freely of her time and advice to the writing of this book. From the first printing to the present, she has offered her experience to this project.

Thanks to Karen Phillips for the cover design and the maps.

Along the way, I've met many others who have encouraged and helped me with this work. I especially thank Scott Daniels and Elerina Aldamar at the Oregon Historical Society, the staff at the Portland Archives and Records Center (PARC), Meg Langford at the OHSU Historical Collections and Archives Library, and the staff of the Multnomah County Library.

INTRODUCTION

FLIP A COIN, name a city: the story that many Portlanders recognize as the event that gave our city its name. It's the story of two men, each wanting to name the new settlement after their own hometown. The guy from Portland, Maine—Pettygrove—won the toss or we would have been called Boston, the city which Lovejoy called home. The names of these two men, along with others like them, wound up on the streets of Northwest Portland in what we now call the Alphabet District and the Pearl District.

For some time, "The Clearing" had been a convenient stopping

The White Stage sign at the western end of the Burnside Bridge is the first thing that many of us see as we enter Northwest Portland. It was at this site that Captain Couch and Flanders built one of the first wharves in the city for their shipping ventures. The area around the waterfront marks the historic beginning of the two districts.

off point between the trading posts of Fort Vancouver and Oregon City, both well-established settlements on the Columbia and Willamette Rivers. There was little evidence that the area that was to become Portland was inhabited. The traveler Jesse Applegate stopped at The Clearing in 1843 and recalls his visit at a much later date:

The first planks for the Great Plank Road were "laid near this spot in September 1851." (The plaque, placed by the Lang Syne Society, is in the South Park Blocks across from the Oregon Historical Society.)

"We landed on the west shore, and went into camp on the high bank where there was thick underbrush. No one lived there and the place had no name, there was nothing to show that the place had ever been visited except a small log hut near the river, and a broken mast of a ship leaning against the high bank…We were then actually encamped on the site of the city of Portland, but there was no prophet with us to tell of the beautiful city that was to take the place of the gloomy forest."[1]

As is turned out, in that same year the first pioneers who were serious about settling here arrived and staked a claim. Shipping captains followed close behind and soon determined that the location was better suited for commerce than others up and down the river. Portland was set to take off.

The historian Percy Maddux offers three reasons for the first Portland boom. Opportunities for trade and commerce expanded rapidly as the California Gold Rush accelerated the flow of people westward. The building of the Great Plank Road (today's Canyon Road) made possible the transport of produce and goods from the valley to the city. And lastly, Portland was home to the first tannery west of the Rocky Mountains, filling a great demand for leather goods as thousands of Americans were on the move in search of riches.[2]

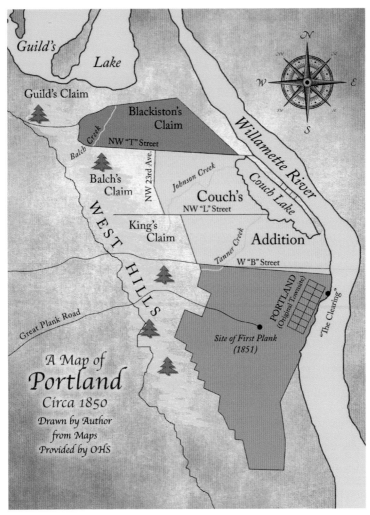

In the early days, Portland looked something like this on a map.

Northwest Portland was bounded on the east by the Willamette River and to the west by the West Hills. On the south the area touched on the original town settlement and to the north it extended to Guild's Lake.

Much of the land was forested and as the forest was cleared, the stumps that remained gave the city the nickname Little Stumptown, still celebrated today with a coffee label. Three creeks ran through it and emptied into two lakes.

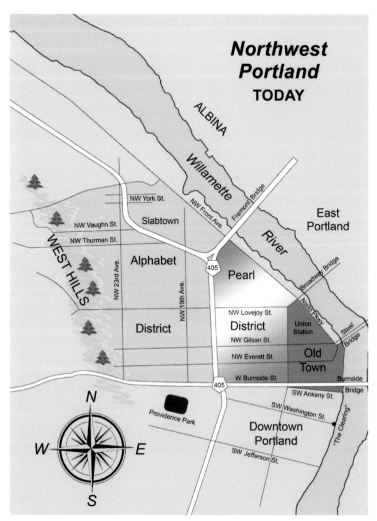

Northwest Portland as it looks on a map today. The boundaries are much the same, but you will not find Guild's Lake, Couch Lake, or the three creeks. See Note at the end of the Introduction, page 11.

Soon the land was platted, first into 200' x 200' blocks and later, west of 19th Street (now 19th Avenue) blocks were expanded so the upper crust could have more room to build their mansions. And build they did. There is an entire book, *Nineteenth Street*, which captures the display of early Portland opulence.[3] By the late 1800s Portland was the third wealthiest city, per capita, in the world.[4]

This brings us to 1891. Up until then the streets in this corner of Portland went, south to north, from A to Z—well, almost to Z. But changes were in the air. Portland was growing and it reached across the Willamette River to merge with the cities of East Portland and Albina.

Confusion over street names was immediate and everywhere. The well-known Portland historian, Eugene Snyder, notes that there were no fewer than twelve "A" Streets, twelve "B" Streets and nine "Cedar" Streets.[5] It fell to the mayor, William Spencer Mason, to appoint a committee to resolve this dilemma. The city employee entrusted with heading up this task was Douglas W. Taylor. His title: Superintendent of Streets.

Under his guidance the committee decided to honor "men who have been identified with Portland and its history."[6] We have been given no insight into the criteria used to choose these names, but we do know that there was competition for many of the letters. While Couch had no rivals, even Lovejoy had to be weighed against Lewis. Pettygrove and Vaughn each had four contenders.[7] And "S" Street was named Scott Street for about a month, before it was changed to Savier.[8]

After much deliberation they submitted the results that history has dubbed "The Great Street Renaming of 1891." It was a monumental effort. The Portland Office of Transportation documented at least 582 name changes throughout the city on January 12, 1892.[9] Each street received an entry that looked like this.[10]

> That "C" street in Couch's Addition to the City of Portland be changed and hereafter known as Couch street.

(Courtesy of Portland Archives and Records Center) (PARC)

Fortunately for the reader, and the writer, we are only dealing here with a slightly abbreviated alphabet! In Northwest Portland, the results are known to us today as the Alphabet District and more recently, the Pearl District. The stories of the worthy men (and yes, they were all men) who were so honored follow.

⁓

NOTE: When looking at the map of modern-day Portland, it might do well to go over several terms that are in use around here today.

In the mid-19th century, the streets in Northwest Portland were laid out in alphabetical order and ran east to west from the Willamette River to the West Hills. The streets run through both what became known as the Alphabet District and the much newer Pearl District.

Interstate 405 cuts through the middle of all of this. The area to the west retained the name Alphabet District, while the portion east of I-405 to the Willamette River became known as the Pearl District. To break it down further, Old Town is carved out of the Pearl District near the waterfront, and the northern part of the Alphabet District is historically known as Slabtown. Jane Comerford, in her comprehensive book on Northwest Portland history, dates the use of the term Pearl District to the late 1980s and credits art gallery director Thomas Augustine with the first mention of the word to designate the area.[11]

THE STREETS

PORTLAND, OREGON. THE METROPOLIS OF THE PACIFIC NORTHWEST.

Northwest Portland in the era of the Great Street Renaming (as depicted in The West Shore Magazine, *1888. (Courtesy of OHS)*

$\mathcal{A}$ IS FOR ANKENY

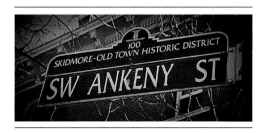

Captain Alexander Postlewaite Ankeny was a soldier, a miner, an adventurer, and the man who gave birth to Portland's market culture. He arrived here in the 1850s and made his fortune in the cattle business and later mining throughout the Pacific Northwest.[1] After establishing himself as a prominent member of the growing community he served on the city council before running, unsuccessfully, for mayor in 1859.

Ankeny had purchased some property on the Willamette River; he had lots of money and he wanted to build a market. In 1872 he did, and it cost him $100,000.[2] The result was the New Market. It was such a magnificent structure that

The arches pictured, at Ankeny Plaza, are the originals. They were salvaged and restored in the 1980s by the Friends of Cast Iron Architecture.

ANKENY ARCADE

Capt. Alexander Ankeny (1813–1891).

it became known as the Renaissance Palace, with a 1,200-seat theater, grander than any other north of San Francisco. The market had offices, a gym, a social club, and spots for 28 retailers.

The theater hosted General Ulysses Grant and booked a boxing exhibition featuring the world heavyweight champion, John L. Sullivan. The market remained a city social hub for many years, but as the city demographics shifted to the west it fell into disrepair and ceased operations in the mid-1880s.

The captain then sold his Portland properties and spent his final years tending to his lucrative Sterling Mine Company in southern Oregon. Ankeny died in Salem in 1891.[3]

Voodoo Doughnut has found a home on Ankeny Street.

SW ANKENY STREET **TODAY**

Ankeny, the only street in the Alphabet District with a SW address, is a short and narrow street and a busy center of activity.[4] A vibrant market life thrives under the graceful arches that recall an earlier grandeur. The Saturday Market is "nationally recognized as the largest continuously operating open-air arts and crafts market in the country."[5] Look for several markers around the plaza that talk about the beginnings of the market.

Skidmore Fountain, a popular gathering spot (SW 1st), Dan and Louis Oyster Bar (SW 2nd), Voodoo Doughnut (SW 3rd).

$\mathcal{B}$ IS FOR BURNSIDE

DAN WYMAN BURNSIDE is the gentleman whose name was given to this street. He arrived in Portland from Vermont in 1852 after a brief stopover in California where he searched for gold. He owned a flour mill where "B" Street met Front Street. He answered the call of civic duty and served for a time on the city council and as a volunteer fireman. In an early version of "it's who you know" Mr. Burnside put himself on the map by marrying Jane Davis, daughter of Portland's first justice of the peace, and partnering with another prominent settler, Thomas Savier.[1]

Dan Wyman Burnside (1825–1887).[2] (Courtesy of OHS)

Portlanders today know Burnside Street as a major east-west arterial that divides the city between north and south, connects the city to the east over the Burnside Bridge, and on the west to the Tualatin Plains. In earlier times people knew it as the best street to get a drink and more.

At Erickson's Saloon "three hundred men could line up along its vast bars—one of them measured 684

The plaque is on the original Erickson's Saloon at NW 2nd and Burnside.

feet. Loggers, railroad workers, miners and sailors poured into the neighborhood to spend their hard-earned wages there."[3] With good reason, Erickson's Saloon became the most famous bar in the Pacific Northwest.

It was from this "Old Town" that tales arose of men being "shanghai'd" to serve on merchant ships. And one can still tour the underground tunnels that spawned these stories and drink the beer that recalls its history. Ever since, Burnside has struggled with an image as the underbelly of Portland. Eugene Snyder notes that "this reputation was so opprobrious that it became almost impossible for an impeccable business firm with an address on Burnside Street to be taken seriously."[4]

Dan W. Burnside passed away in 1887 at the age of 62.

Shanghai'd IPA from Old Town Brewing, NW 2nd and Davis.

W BURNSIDE STREET **TODAY**

W Burnside is the gateway to Portland's Chinatown and Japan Town (Nihonmachi), Erickson-Fritz Apartments (NW 2nd), Powell's Books (NW 10th), Henry's 12th Street Tavern (NW 12th), McMenamins Crystal Ballroom (NW 13th), Providence Park, just south of W Burnside (NW 18th), Fred Meyer (NW 20th), Elephant's Deli (NW 22nd), Zupan's Market (NW 23rd).

C IS FOR COUCH
(SAY "KOOCH" IN PORTLAND)

Captain John Heard Couch was one of Portland's founding fathers in the truest sense of the word. Many have argued that it was he more than anyone else who was responsible for the positioning of the city where it is today.

For starters, in 1840 Couch was the first to bring an ocean-going vessel as far as the place that was to become Portland. Soon thereafter, with the utterance "to this point I can bring any ship that can get into the mouth of the great Columbia River,"[1] he determined that

This plaque at what is now the Metropolitan Learning Center on NW Glisan points to one of the many legacies of the Couch Family. The school is adjacent to Couch Park.

Portland, and not Oregon City, was to be the "head of navigation" on the Willamette River.

That settled, he laid claim to a 640-acre tract of land in 1845 that encompassed much of the present-day Pearl District and parts of the Alphabet District. The Donation Land Claim Act of 1850 cemented the claim. When Portland incorporated in 1851 it included 154 acres of Couch's claim and made him one of the largest and wealthiest property owners in Portland.[2] He built his first house at NW 4th and "H" Street, on the west side of a marshy lake that covered about 40 city blocks.[3] The lake came to be called, appropriately, Couch Lake. He was said to shoot ducks for dinner from his front porch.

We cannot leave the good captain without noting that he was married and fathered four daughters with his wife Caroline.

The following piece of local lore is recounted by historian E. Kimbark MacColl: "How should a young man assure his future

The Couch house at NW 4th and "H."[4] The house is long gone, but some of the furniture has been preserved and can be found in the Couch Bedroom of the Pittock Mansion.[5]

prosperity in Portland?" was the question. The answer: "Join Trinity Episcopal Church . . . and marry a Couch." [6] We will see that more than one pioneer took that advice and Couch's heirs have populated the finer streets of Portland for many years.

Captain John Heard Couch (1811–1870) and his wife Caroline.[7] She was active in extending the plat of Couch's Addition to the north and west after his death.

Captain Couch was held in great esteem in his city. When he died of typhoid pneumonia in 1870 [8] *The Morning Oregonian* noted that "the funeral cortege was never excelled in Portland . . . The banks closed . . . and all combined to pay respect and do honor to the revered pioneer and beloved citizen."[9]

Trinity Episcopal Cathedral.

NW COUCH STREET **TODAY**

Pearl Bakery (NW 9th), Sur La Table (NW 11th), Whole Foods Market (NW 12th).

$\mathcal{D}$IS FOR DAVIS

LONE FIR PIONEER CEMETERY is the resting place of many of Portland's earliest settlers. Information on the *findagrave.com* website for Major Anthony L. Davis gives us a good outline of the life of this Indiana gentleman.

We learn that Davis was among those who helped organize the first public school in Portland. "He was one of the most zealous advocates of Portland's free school system,"[1] and in 1851 he became its first director.

The first teacher appointed to that school was a 22-year-old Canadian named Mr. John Outhouse, hired at a salary of $100 per month. This was apparently not a living wage at that time, as he had to work a second job on the docks to support his family.[2] The textbooks he used to teach his 20 students: "*Saunder's Readers, Goodrich's Geographies, Thompson's Arithmetics* and *Bullion's Grammar.*"[3]

Major Anthony Davis. (Courtesy of OHS)[4]

Davis's service in the cause of public education and his election, in 1854, as Portland's first justice of the peace were enough to change the name of "D" Street to Davis Street. In 1858 he was also appointed circuit judge.

In a revealing letter to a friend dated March 1862, in the midst of the Civil War, Major Davis railed against the Abolitionists, concluding that "if holding these views" makes me a traitor, then "I'm a traitor!" He went on the say that the war "can have no other result than to engulpf us in eternal ruin."[5]

Davis's youngest daughter married the Burnside we met on "B" Street. A descendant identified Major Davis as his "3G grandfather" and placed flowers at the gravesite as recently as 2012.

Anthony L. Davis (1794-1866), grave marker at Lone Fir Cemetery.

NW DAVIS STREET **TODAY**

Gerding Theater at the Armory (NW 11th), Deschutes Brewery (NW 11th).

$\mathcal{E}$ IS FOR EVERETT

EDWARD EVERETT was favored with a street name for his activities with the Northwest Fire and Marine Insurance Company and his contributions to the Oregon National Guard. Born in Boston in 1856, he arrived in Portland in 1883 and stayed. He was a businessman and a colonel who commanded the 3rd Oregon Infantry Regiment, headquartered in Portland.

The Lovejoy Columns at NW 10th and Everett were painted almost 70 years ago by a Greek immigrant who worked in the rail yards, Tom Stefopoulos. When the Lovejoy Ramp was torn down in 1999, some of the columns were salvaged and two placed near their original location.[1]

In 1891, the year of the Great Street Renaming, East Portland and Albina were consolidated with Portland into one city.

In celebration of the event, Colonel Everett was at the head of the parade, representing his regiment. At the time, the modest colonel is said to have told *The Oregonian* that the naming committee had trouble finding a prominent citizen whose last name started with "E" so they reluctantly named it after him.[2]

He resigned from his regimental duties in 1896 but was called back to duty with the National Guard during the Spanish-American War. Upon his second retirement, in 1902, he was presented with a sword (right) "for a popular officer" by the officers of the Third Regiment.[3]

When *The Oregonian* published its 1921 series on street names it said that "Colonel Everett, although not in the best of health, is still actively engaged in his insurance business, and is at his office frequently."[4] He died in 1937.

SWORD FOR A POPULAR OFFICER.

Colonel Edward Everett with sword, The Evening Telegram, *August 23, 1902.*

NW EVERETT STREET **TODAY**

NW Everett is a busy one-way street and an important thoroughfare that leads east to the Steel Bridge. Lan Su Chinese Garden (NW 3rd), Tanner Creek Tavern (NW 9th), World Foods (NW 9th), Nuvrei Bakery (NW 10th), Restoration Hardware (NW 23rd), Pottery Barn (NW 23rd).

$\mathcal{F}$ IS FOR FLANDERS

CAPTAIN GEORGE HALL FLANDERS was, like Couch, from Newburyport, Massachusetts, and he had the sea in his blood. He came to Portland in 1849 on a ship captained by Couch, who was by then also his brother-in-law. They set up business together on the waterfront and built a wharf between "B" and "D" Streets.[1] Couch made his ship *Madonna* available to Flanders for trade between Portland and California.

And a handsome trade it was. The historian Eugene Snyder provides us with an example, from April 1847, of just how profitable this trade could be. The bark *Columbia* carried 900 barrels of flour from the

Centennial Mills, first known as Crown Mills, sits on the Willamette River at the top of Fields Park. It was built by Balfour, Guthrie and Co. in 1910, by which time Portland was already recognized as the flour mill center of the Pacific Northwest.[2]

Columbia River to San Francisco. A barrel of flour cost $6 in Oregon and sold for $15 in California, showing a profit of over $8,000. Ships could make the round trip in about two months and the return journey, of course, also proved profitable. So it is not difficult to account for the rise of the "merchant princes," as they became known.[4]

Captain George H. Flanders (1821–1892). (Courtesy of OHS)[3]

Soon Flanders' wealth placed him squarely among the city elite. By the 1880s the merchant princes were moving away from the waterfront and to the wider blocks west of NW 19th. It was there, at the corner of "F" Street, that Flanders built one of the grand old mansions of Portland at a cost of $40,000.[5]

But if the sea provided his livelihood, Flanders' legacy is also tied to the rails. Those of us who go to sleep to the rhythm of the freight trains can thank the captain for his pivotal role in promoting the railroads. When it came time to build the terminus we know as Union Station, it was Flanders who contributed the largest sum of money. And it was Flanders and Couch who donated the land on which the depot was built.[7]

Flanders Mansion c. 1870. (Courtesy of OHS)[6]

Steam Locomotive SP 4449, shown here leaving Union Station, is now housed at the Oregon Rail Heritage Center. The engine was fully restored for the 1976 Bicentennial Celebration, and is "the only remaining operable "streamlined" steam locomotive of the Art Deco era."[8]

Flanders died at his residence in 1892, a year after "F" Street was named in his honor. *The Oregonian*: "Captain George H. Flanders is confined to his home by a paralytic stroke. His condition is critical and there is no hope for his recovery."[9] The obituary went on to write of the captain in glowing terms: "his was a character so pure that it was almost beyond human comprehension . . . a life spent in good actions to others."[10]

Temple Beth Israel stands on the grounds of the Flanders Mansion. The stone walls and the trees are from Flanders' time.

These virtues may account for his incarnation as the very good and pious Ned Flanders in *The Simpsons*.

G IS FOR GLISAN

*(Purists insist that his name should rhyme with "listen,"
but the pronunciation of the street named for him has
long ago morphed into "gleeson").*

RODNEY GLISAN was one of two doctors whose names were added to the district's streets. He hailed from Baltimore and after graduating from the University of Maryland he served for a time as an Army surgeon. His sojourn in the military was exhaustively chronicled, complete with illustrations, in his *Journal of Army Life*. It spanned the years 1850–1858 when Glisan was posted throughout the western territories, including a time at Port Orford in Oregon.

When he moved to Portland in about 1862 he did two things that helped pave his road to success: He married Elizabeth, one of the daughters of Captain Couch, and joined Trinity Episcopal Church.

*Dr. Rodney Glisan (1827–1890).[2]
(Courtesy of OHSU)*

Dr. Glisan went on to achieve prominence as a member of the American Medical Association and as a professor at Willamette University's School of Medicine.[1] He lectured extensively in the United States as well as Europe and published medical texts that were widely circulated.

The memoirs of his sojourn in Europe entitled *Two Years in Europe* are still in circulation. Dr. Glisan's résumé included the first amputation of the shoulder and thigh in the Pacific Northwest.[3]

His medical skills were not able, however, to postpone his sudden death at the age of 63. He had participated in a meeting at Trinity Church and returned to his home at NW 18th and "I" Street in good health. Three hours later he passed away of apoplexy or "something of that kind."[4] Upon his passing, his considerable collection of books was donated to the library of what would become the Oregon Health and Sciences University (OHSU).[5]

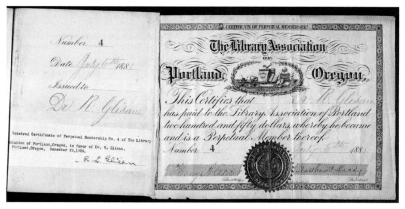

Certificate showing Dr. Glisan's lifetime membership in the Library Association of Portland as of 1881. It cost him $250. Before the library was opened to the public, only members could access the collection.[6]

NW GLISAN STREET **TODAY**

Pacific Northwest College of Art (NW Broadway), Canopy by Hilton (NW 9th), Blick Arts (NW 11th), Andina Restaurant (NW 13th), Ace Hardware (NW 16th), Mission Theater (NW 17th), Couch Park (NW 19th), Metropolitan Learning Center (NW 20th), Trader Joe's (NW 21st).

$\mathscr{H}$IS FOR HOYT

RICHARD HOYT (1817–1862) was a seafaring captain and an enterprising businessman. He came to Portland late in life and died early in life but left his mark.

Hoyt had already made a career of sailing between New York and England for several years. There he met young William Irving, our next street name, and they later struck up a business partnership.

But it was the era of gold fever and before settling here, Hoyt stopped off in California. He found work sailing out of San Francisco. One such voyage is recounted by a passenger in 1849: "The bark *Toulon* was commanded by Captain Richard Hoyt . . . cabin passage was $80, deck passage $60 and it took 34 days from San Francisco harbor to the mouth of the Columbia River."[1]

Captain Richard Hoyt.

When he arrived in Portland for good, he carried passengers on his steamboat, the *Black Hawk*, between Portland and Oregon City.[2] He later captained the steamboat *Multnomah*, the fastest vessel on the river. It made the trip between Portland and Vancouver in one hour and twenty minutes—about what it takes now in bad traffic! The steamboat caused much public enthusiasm and inspired this poem from 1851 on the occasion of her first passage up the Willamette River:

"There comes the Multnomah*! Success to the steamer*
Sweet sounding her music, high floating her streamer;
The sound of her paddles the hills serenading,
And her smoke high aloft into vapor is fading.
There comes the Multnomah *shout fifty glad voices;*
Each heart beats with rapture, each bosom rejoices,
Her structure so firm, yet buoyant and airy
She skims o'er the waves like a sylph or a fairy.
There comes the Multnomah*, we greet her with pleasure,*
The choicest of welcomes to her is extended,
Because with her welfare our interests are blended."[3]

Later still, he purchased two other river-going vessels for service on the Columbia River. In 1857 he founded the Columbia Steam Navigation Company which plied the river and tapped into the lucrative gold mining industry as far away as Idaho.

The steamship Multnomah *at the foot of Washington Street, Portland, 1853.*[4]

Sadly, after a harrowing trip in mid-winter on the above-mentioned *Multnomah* Captain Hoyt fell ill from "severe exposure" and did not recover. He was buried in Lone Fir Cemetery at the young age of 44.[5]

NW HOYT STREET **TODAY**

U.S. Post Office, Main Branch (NW 9th), William Temple House (NW 20th).

I IS FOR IRVING

WHEN WILLIAM IRVING (1816–1872) arrived in Portland in 1849 he was already a seasoned sailor. By the time he left for Canada in 1859, he had earned the title "King of the River."

Born in Scotland, he found his way to New York when he was only 15, where he met Richard Hoyt. He signed on to Hoyt's brig *Tuscany* and sailed with him between New York and England.

Once in Portland, he turned his attention to steamboats. He brought the steamship *Multnomah* from the East Coast and gave over

Captain William Irving, Sr.[2]

its operation to Hoyt. For himself, Irving purchased the smaller *Eagle* and put it on a passenger run between Portland and Oregon City, charging five dollars a head for the round trip.[1]

Irving may actually be better known today for the part of the city just east of the Broadway Bridge called Irvington. When his name was chosen to represent "I" Street, two streets on the east side that

34

were already named after him had to change their names: thus Irving Street became Knott Street and Irvington Street became Fremont Street.[3]

Irving's successful career in Portland did not keep him here for long. Within ten years he had moved to Vancouver, British Columbia, where he became a prominent citizen of New Westminster until his death in 1872. His life was chronicled by his granddaughter, Mary Aline Cox, in *Saga of a Seafarer*, published in Canada.

The Victorian house, relocated to NE 12th Avenue, where Elizabeth Irving lived out her life with her daughter Lizzy Spencer. (Courtesy of Chris Thomas)

His widow, Elizabeth, however, returned to Portland where she remarried, went through an ugly divorce, and then lived out her life with her daughter in the stately Victorian house shown here. The house has been moved but, with modifications, is still standing on NE 12th Avenue in the Irvington district of Northeast Portland.

This home, built in 1884 at NW 18th and Irving Street, is one of several historic houses on Irving Street, which are part of the Couch Family Investment Development.[4]

NW IRVING STREET **TODAY**

Union Station (NW 6th), Ecotrust Building (NW 10th), Irving Kitchen (NW 13th), Papa Haydn (NW 23rd).

J IS FOR JOHNSON

ARTHUR HARRISON JOHNSON (1830–1894) was born in London and came to the United States with his family when he was a young man. His father was a butcher who taught the trade to his son. The family settled in Wisconsin but Arthur moved on to Portland in 1852.

Upon his arrival he set up a slaughterhouse next to a stream that became known as Johnson Creek, at NW 23rd and "F" Street.[1] (The creek emptied into the old Couch Lake and has long since been rerouted underground with its sister, Tanner Creek.) He went into business with Richard Perkins, and they remained partners for 10 years before Perkins retired and Johnson struck out on his own.

His primary business was wholesale, but when Ankeny's New Market opened in 1872, Johnson set up a retail business there. *The Oregonian* noted that "he was the heaviest dealer in meats in the city, with sales reaching $200,000–$400,000 per year."[2]

Ad from The Oregonian, *Aug 26, 1876.*[3]

The Johnson Estate.[4] The Johnsons raised 14 children on their King's Hill Estate. (Courtesy of OHS)

Johnson later expanded his interests to include real estate and became a prominent landowner in the Goose Hollow neighborhood. He contributed to the cause of education by donating a parcel of land for the construction of St. Helen's Hall, an elite school for girls and a forerunner of Oregon Episcopal School.[5]

For his residence, he chose a spot on King's Hill, where he built a sprawling estate. He and his wife, Cordelia St. Clair, made their home at 193 St. Clair Avenue—named in her honor—and raised 14 children. The elegant mansion and surrounding buildings were demolished between 1926 and 1932 to make room for the Vista Avenue Apartments.[6]

Mr. Johnson lived until 1894, long enough to see his name go up on "J" Street.

NW JOHNSON STREET TODAY

Jamison Park (NW 10th), Heartline Apartments (NW 13th), REI (NW 14th).

K IS FOR KEARNEY

ACCORDING to an *Oregonian* article as late as 1921, there seemed to be some doubt among old-time Portlanders as to which Kearney this street was named after. But most historians have settled on Edward Smith Kearney. He was a Philadelphian who was appointed U.S. marshal by President Garfield in 1881, at which time he moved to Portland.

His singular distinction as marshal: he sent the first three prisoners to McNeil Island Penitentiary which had just opened up in what was then part of the Washington Territory. Their crimes: two had been convicted of selling whiskey to Native Americans

Portrait of Edward Kearney in Multnomah County (Central) Library.

and received twenty months and eighteen months. The other got twelve months for robbing a store at Fort Walla Walla.[1]

But his stint as a U.S. marshal was probably not enough to earn him a street with his name. Following his years in law enforcement he became a successful businessman; so successful that his occupation in the Portland directory was listed as "capitalist."[2] With his newfound wealth he contributed generously to the Portland Library and the Children's Home.

Upon the occasion of this death, his good friend Judge Whalley allowed that at times he was quite "rusty in manner," but under the surface he was loving and tender. As a marshal, he was honest to a fault and managed his records with great care and accuracy. *The Morning Oregonian* adds this glimpse of his personality, saying that "he is remem-

Edward S. Kearney (1830–1897).

bered for a taciturn disposition given to eccentricities."[3] His will stated that he be buried alone, and so he was, in an impressive mausoleum in Riverview Cemetery, Portland.[4]

Kearney had a reputation as a tough guy and a tough enforcer. At the penitentiary he required his prisoners to work all day, every day, except Sunday.[5] It is no accident that he is featured as a bully in the long-running TV series *The Simpsons*, as we will see in the next segment.

NW KEARNEY STREET **TODAY**

On Deck Sports Bar (NW 14th), Radio Cab (NW 16th), Cafe Nell (NW 20th).

Bart Simpson on the sidewalk, SW 18th and Salmon.

NW PORTLAND & "THE SIMPSONS" CONNECTION

THE SIMPSONS are creeping into the narrative so it may be appropriate to stop and pay our respects to their creator, Portlander Matt Groening. This etching of Bart Simpson can be found on the sidewalk in front of Groening's alma mater, Lincoln High School. The likeness, however, was not drawn by him as was first thought, but by another Portland artist named Matt Wuerker, in 1995.[1] Bart's name does not derive from a Portland street but the Alphabet District is responsible for naming at least four of *The Simpsons'* characters. For introducing these street names to a worldwide audience we thank Mr. Groening.

We've already met George Flanders, whose first name became Ned, the pious one. He says things like "Say your prayers, Simpson . . . because the schools can't force you like they should." And "I've done everything the Bible says—even the stuff that contradicts the other stuff."[2]

Edward Kearney, appropriately, became one of the school bullies. The bully's first name, Kearney, was taken from the street; his surname in *The Simpsons* is Zzyzwicx (pronounced "jeez-wich"). He is a bully because he's a Cubs fan.[3]

Lovejoy is next. His first name is Timothy but he is usually known as just Rev. Lovejoy. He passes on to members of the Western Branch of American Reform Presbylutheran congregation such gems as "Once something has been approved by the government, it's no longer immoral."[4]

Finally, there is the womanizing mayor of Springfield, Mr. Quimby. As mayor, his worthy quotes include the following: "You can't seriously want to ban alcohol."[5]

Portland, the city acknowledged as the reigning craft beer capital of the country, no doubt concurs. Henry Weinhard, whose namesake brew house on Burnside is pictured here, was an early giant in the beer industry. The surrounding area is now called the Brewery Blocks.

Henry's 12th Street Tavern, NW 12th and Burnside on the site of the old Weinhard Brewery.

Two other names have less direct connections to *The Simpsons*.

Montgomery Burns, Homer's boss, is a combination of two parts of the district—the huge neon Montgomery Park sign in the northwest corner (formerly the Montgomery Ward store), and Burnside Street.

And finally, the last name of Homer's half-brother, Herb Powell, is taken from the prominent bookstore, Powell's City of Books, that stands on W Burnside at the entrance to the Pearl District.

$\mathcal{L}$ IS FOR LOVEJOY

Asa Lawrence Lovejoy, (1808–1882) is generally thought to be the first of several city founders, for he registered the first claim on the land was to be Portland. In 1843 Lovejoy and a fellow pioneer named William Overton were canoeing up the Willamette River between Fort Vancouver and Oregon City. They stopped on the western bank at a spot known as "The Clearing." Overton liked it well enough that he decided to stake a claim. Historians have long held that Overton offered Lovejoy half of the 640-acre land claim for the required

Asa Lovejoy (1808–1882).
(Courtesy of OHS)[1]

25-cent filing fee. Recent research, spearheaded by Portlander Randall Trowbridge, casts new light on this transaction. It was not Overton's lack of a quarter but his need for Lovejoy's legal services which motivated him to part with half of his claim. In short, he paid for Lovejoy's expertise. (See the chapter on Overton for more details of this rewriting of a small but significant piece of Portland history.)

Not long after, Overton sold his

half of the claim to Pettygrove. That left Lovejoy and Pettygrove to plat and develop the early blocks of Portland and, of course, to name it. At an occasion in the living room of the Francis Ermatinger House in

Francis Ermatinger House, Oregon City.

Oregon City, Lovejoy of Boston and Pettygrove of Portland, Maine, were having a light-hearted discussion about what to name the new town. Each favored his hometown. Their solution was to flip a coin, making two out of three "heads" the winner. So out of Pettygrove's pocket came an 1835 Matron Head copper penny.[2] Lovejoy tossed first and the coin came up two tails. Pettygrove's coin toss came up two heads. "The Clearing" had a name: Portland.

Lovejoy went on to become mayor of Oregon City, a general in the Cayuse War, the first speaker of the Oregon House of Representatives, part owner of the Oregon Telegraph newspaper, and VP of the Willamette Steam Navigation Company. He spent most of his career in Oregon City but moved to Portland in 1873.

Late in life his health failed and he suffered a fall from a railway bridge. Lovejoy passed away in 1882 at his home, not far from The Clearing he had claimed almost 40 years earlier. He left behind his wife, Elizabeth McGary, two sons and two daughters. Lovejoy was buried in Lone Fir Pioneer Cemetery.

Lovejoy has found his honored place in Portland many times over. Besides the street, there's a bakery, a park, a fountain, the Asa Apartments, the Lovejoy Columns, a soon-to-be constructed Lovejoy Square, and of course the beloved Simpsons character, Reverend Timothy Lovejoy.

NW LOVEJOY STREET **TODAY**

Lovejoy Bakers (NW 10th), Safeway (NW 13th), Nossa Familia (NW 13th), Legacy Good Samaritan Hospital (NW 22nd), Blue Star Donuts (NW 23rd)

$\mathcal{M}$ IS FOR MARSHALL

WE'RE IN LINE with most historians if we choose John Marshall as the "M" Street namesake. Others who vied for the honor were a George and Thomas. But a 1921 article in *The Oregonian*, written while Marshall was still alive, makes the case for John.[1]

John "Johnny" Marshall lived a long life, much of it on the river. He came to the United States from England at the tender age of nine and following a brief stopover in Chicago, came west with his family. By the time he was 16 he was working at a machine shop in Oregon City run by Smith and Moffett.

But after two years he tired of that and took to the water.

John Marshall (1837-1924).[3]

Anecdotally, he is said to have refused to pay the $5 fare from Portland to Oregon City on the steamship *Eagle*, choosing instead to walk. He arrived at about the same time as the boat! He vowed to do better.[2] He first worked as an engineer on the steamboat *Enterprise* which ran between Oregon City and Corvallis on the Willamette River. In an attempt to recruit passengers and beat his

The steamship, Enterprise.

competition, the story goes that the steamboat carried a five-gallon jug of whiskey on board![4]

Forty-seven years later, as the chief engineer of the Willamette Transportation Company, it was said that he had travelled more river miles than any other engineer.[5] During those years Marshall was linked with some of Portland's most wealthy and powerful shipping magnates, Capt. John Ainsworth and Jacob Kamm. He even counted among his acquaintances Ulysses S. Grant and was later invited to visit him at the White House.

When he retired from the river in 1902 he shifted his financial interests to the Oregon Coast and for a time was president of the Newport Navigation Co. and part owner of the steamer *Newport*.

He lived out his last years at 827 Marshall Street, the street bearing his name.[6] He was survived by his wife of more than 60 years, Sarah Davis (no relation to Davis Street), with whom he had five children.

John "Johnny" Marshall, age 82. (Courtesy of Wikipedia)

NW MARSHALL STREET **TODAY**

Marriott Residence Inn (NW 9th), Tanner Springs Park (NW 10th & 11th), Via Delizia (NW 11th), Bridgeport Brew Pub (NW 13th, Portland's oldest craft brewery), Pok Pok NW (NW 16th).

$\mathcal{N}$ IS FOR NORTHRUP

EDWARD J. NORTHRUP (1834–1883) was a businessman who came to Portland at age 15 from New York. A shipwreck on the coast of Chile almost cost his entire family their lives, but they made it here in 1849. After apprenticing with his father for several years, he went into business with J. M. Blossom and opened a hardware store known as Blossom & Northrup. The firm prospered and after several incarnations, Northrup brought J. G. Chown into his firm.[1] The Chown Hardware name became prominent in Portland; a Chown hardware store still stands at the corner of NW 16th and Flanders.

Northrup spoke often of a Lt. Ulysses Grant, in those days the post quartermaster at Fort Vancouver, as a customer of his hardware store.[2] Grant returned to Portland after becoming a general (see Ankeny) but we have no record of him meeting up again with Northrup.

Northrup's business prospered, first on Yamhill and then at a store on Front Street between Salmon and Main. It was there, only months after moving, that an unfortunate incident took Northrup's life. In 1883, while

Ad from The Oregonian, *July 25, 1878.*[3]

*Above: Northrup House, 730 Madison Street,
c. 1870. (Courtesy of OHS)*[4]
Right: Edward J. Northrup.[5]

working in his new store, he fell through a trap door that had been left open accidentally, landing 20 feet below with a fractured skull. He died within a few hours.

*Northrup and Blossom-Fitch Building
SW Naito Parkway and Yamhill.*

Northrup "was one of the men whom the community can least afford to spare."[6] His imprint on the young town was strong and earned him a street name.

His warehouse, built in 1858 and now known now as the Northrup and Blossom-Fitch Building, was the only structure in Portland's Yamhill Historic District to survive the Great Fire of 1873.[7] It stands on the corner of SW Naito (Front Ave.) and SW Yamhill Street, an important example of early commercial architecture.

NW NORTHRUP STREET **TODAY**

Streetcar Line from the Pearl District to shops on NW 23rd. Hoyt Property Management (NW 10th), Fields Bar & Grill (NW 11th), Carlita's (NW 11th), Les Schwab (NW 19th), Northrup Station Hotel (NW 20th), Paley's Place Bistro (NW 21st).

O IS FOR OVERTON

FOR A PIONEER who figures so prominently in the early story of Portland and who is credited with staking the first claim on this land, little information has been available on William P. Overton. Early assessments of him were dismissive. In 1875 Oregon Senator Nesmith called him a "desperate, rollicking fellow."[1] Historian Harvey Scott offers the following: "This man Overton stalks through the twilight of these early annals like a phantom of tradition, so little is known of his history, character, and fate."[2]

That is changing, however, as history enthusiast Randall Trowbridge digs deeply into the life of Overton. He has traced Overton's roots to Alabama and later to Missouri and has found his signature on documents in Alabama, Missouri, and Oregon.[3]

Overton's signature (Courtesy Oregon State Archives/Randall Trowbridge)[4]

Long before Portland was Portland, Oregon City was an established trading post at the falls of the Willamette River. Halfway to the Hudson's Bay Company post at Ft. Vancouver, a spot on the riverbank known as "The Clearing" served as a convenient rest stop for travelers to and fro, and for Native American canoes before that.

On just such a trip in 1843 Overton rested his canoe at The Clearing. His traveling partner was Asa Lovejoy. Historians routinely refer to Overton as a "drifter" but on that day he demonstrated considerable foresight by envisioning a town on that clearing. He told Lovejoy that he wanted to file a claim.

There was not much to recommend the unfriendly site. Even several years later it was

One of the earliest photographs of Portland, 1851. (Courtesy of OHS)[5]

described by diarist Elizabeth Dixon Smith Geer in the following manner: "We traveled four or five miles through the thickest woods I ever saw on an intolerable bad road. These woods are infested with wild cats, panthers, bears and wolves."[6]

It's here that the story strays from the more conventional narrative. The earliest histories of Portland recount that because Overton lacked the required 25-cent fee, Lovejoy filed the claim for the townsite on his behalf and was rewarded with half of that claim. Trowbridge posits that Overton was not the penniless drifter as often portrayed, and offers this explanation from Mrs. Elizabeth McGary Lovejoy (Asa's wife): "he (Overton) had no means to take the legal steps to secure the claim according to law, and offered Lovejoy a half interest in the claim for the expense of recording."

But Overton was not long for "Portland". He tired of making shingles in the soggy Portland winters. Trowbridge reports that Overton went to Honolulu in 1844 and left for Missouri in the spring of 1845. Before leaving, Overton traded his half of the land claim to Francis Pettygrove who then teamed up with Lovejoy to make important improvements to the townsite. The mystery of this first among Portland pioneers is slowly unraveling.

NW OVERTON STREET **TODAY**

Cafe Ovation (NW 10th), Fields Park (NW 11th), Pure Space Event Center and Table Tennis Club (NW 14th).

$\mathcal{P}$IS FOR PETTYGROVE

By now we know Francis William Pettygrove (1812–1887) as the winner of the famous coin toss with Lovejoy that named Portland after his home town back east. Who else was he? Pettygrove moved from Maine to the Oregon Territory in 1843 and worked as a trader. His trade was in wheat, lumber, fish, and fur, and his store was in Oregon City.

Soon after arriving, he purchased Overton's half of the Portland townsite claim and set about, with Asa Lovejoy, to develop the fledgling

town. With Captain John Couch's backing he hired surveyor Thomas Brown, who laid out the city in the unusually small 200-foot-square blocks still seen today. His wife, Sophie, joined him in making another early contribution: in 1846, their second son, Benjamin

Pettygrove (center) with his family. (Courtesy of OHS).[1]

Stark Pettygrove, became the first boy of European descent born in Portland.[2] They built their home, a crude log cabin, at the corner of Front and Washington Streets and built a log store across the street.[3]

The Portland Penny, Pettygrove's 1835 Matron Head copper penny in its display case on the first floor of the Oregon Historical Society.

This store spawned the following tale. When Pettygrove first arrived in "Portland" he had brought a large quantity of red paint hoping to sell it to Native Americans for their war ceremonies. But when he arrived he learned that they made their own paint and had no use for his! He decided to paint his store red and it became known for years as the "Red Store".[4]

Pettygrove developed a lucrative triangular trade between Portland, San Francisco, and Hawaii and within three short years he became one of the wealthiest men in the territory.[5] He built a slaughterhouse on the river and sold his hides to Daniel Lownsdale who had just built the first tannery on the West Coast.[6] Investing $1,800 of his own money, Pettygrove was also instrumental in developing the Great Plank Road (Canyon Road) which allowed goods from the Tualatin Valley to reach the Willamette River.

But by 1851 the California gold rush lured Pettygrove away and he left Oregon for good. While his place in early Portland history is secure, he then headed north and spent the last twenty years of his life developing another city—Port Townsend, Washington—where he died and was buried in 1887.

NOTE: His great-grandson, Frank Pettygrove McIntyre, a life-long resident of Portland, was buried at Lone Fir Cemetery in January 2018.

NW PETTYGROVE STREET **TODAY**

Planet Granite (NW 14th), DoveLewis Animal Hospital (NW 19th), Joe's Cellar (NW 21st), Chapman School chimney and the seasonal nesting of the Vaux's Swifts (NW 26th).

$\mathcal{Q}$ IS FOR QUIMBY

LOT P. W. QUIMBY (1838–1924) WAS AN INNKEEPER from Vermont. Like so many others, he came to Portland via California, stopping to seek his fortune in gold. For a while he was employed in the livery business. He did well and soon made his way into the hospitality business. He built a home at NW 14th and Johnson where he and his wife raised six children.[1]

By the 1870s he had partnered with a Mr. Perkins to purchase the American Exchange Hotel at the corner of Front and Washington Streets. And what was a hotel in Portland, then and now, without a saloon? By 1873 the city boasted 73 retail liquor outlets for a population of 15,000![2]

In this excerpt from *The Oregonian*, the American Exchange Hotel was remembered as a "top-notch hostelry" which served "venison potpie." "Mr. Quimby in those days was a hunter of no mean pretensions, and it is said that he kept his hotel larder well supplied with choice haunches and sirloins of venison, obtained from the then-good hunting grounds on Portland Heights."[3] Quimby may have given birth to Portland's "farm to table" cuisine!

He went on to own the Quimby House at NW 4th and Couch, the best known of his hotels and an establishment which helped earn

QUIMBY HOUSE,

Corner Fourth and C Streets,
PORTLAND, OREGON.

First Class Family Hotel. Only House in
the State with Elevator and Hy-
draulic Fire Apparatus. No
Dark Rooms.

Free Coach to and from the House.

RATES $1 PER DAY,   25 CENTS PER MEAL.
L. P. W. QUIMBY, Propr.

Fifteen Years in the American Exchange Hotel.

Ad from The Oregonian, *1886.*[7]

him a street with his name. The hotel boasted 175 guest rooms, running water (albeit only cold),[4] and the first passenger elevator in the state. A further description notes that the reputation of the hotel had "extended for a great distance on the Pacific coast, the service and accommodation being such as to delight the heart of the traveler."[5]

We get a glimpse of his personal life from a 1921 *Oregonian* article: "Mr. Quimby is still about and although eighty-four years old is seen almost daily. He bears the stamp of the earlier days with his Stetson hat, string bow tie and heavy gold watch chain…lately he has been passing his winters in Los Angeles,"[6] portending another Portland trend.

Lot Porter Woodruff Quimby, known to his friends as L.P.W., died in Seattle in 1924 and was buried in Lone Fir Cemetery in Portland.

Quimby's reputation followed him to *The Simpsons*, where he is the owner of a saloon and the mayor of Springfield.

NOTE: Wayne Quimby, a descendant whom I had the pleasure of meeting, still resides in Northwest Portland. Like his ancestor, he also winters in California.

NW QUIMBY STREET **TODAY**

Play Date PDX (NW 17th), Bull Run Distilling Co. (NW 22nd), Stepping Stone Café (NW 24th), Wallace Park (NW 25th).

$\mathcal{R}$ IS FOR RALEIGH

WE HAVE SPARSE INFORMATION about Albert E. Raleigh. His claim to fame seems to be his position as Deputy Superintendent of Streets—in other words, an assistant to Douglas Taylor, the man charged with renaming the streets in 1891.[1] It was this position that led Snyder to record A. E. Raleigh as the honoree. Raleigh served the department with distinction and was well respected by his superiors. He later worked for the U. S. Customs Service and, in an 1894 city record, is listed as a statistician for the Port of Portland, with an annual salary of $1,400.[2]

The Morning Oregonian relates a good fish story about Mr. Raleigh under the header: "Fished for trout, got suckers."

One weekend Mr. Raleigh and his Customs House buddy Mr. Forbes took a fishing trip to Skamokawa. It seems Forbes went far up stream and caught 30 trout, while our Mr. Raleigh and another friend stayed below and caught 60 suckers.[3]

A closer look shows that at least an equal claim should attach to his father, Patrick Raleigh (1817–1868). *The Oregonian* of 1897 gives substance to this claim with Albert's obituary, which states that the street was named for his father, Patrick. The elder Raleigh, who had come over from Ireland and was said to be related to Sir Walter Raleigh, was a retail merchant who platted the Raleigh Addition to Portland. The claim was a triangular piece of land extending from Stark to Ankeny, and Broadway to 12th. Of interest to sports fans, the historian Joseph Gaston notes that the land claim served as the first baseball field in Portland. Patrick married Mary Louisa Kain, with whom he had 8 children, and they built their house on the block (Broadway and Washington)

A. E. Raleigh (1855–1897).[4]

where the Imperial Hotel (Kimpton Vintage Hotel) now stands. For his business he built one of the first brick structures in Portland, on the southeast corner of First and Stark.

Patrick Raleigh moved his business interests out of Portland later in life and lost his connection to the city. Nevertheless, it may be appropriate to let father and son share the honor, much as they share the grave marker at Mt. Calvary Catholic Cemetery.

William W. Chapman (1808–1892) merits mention here, though his name does not appear on a Northwest street. Chapman was a lawyer, politician, and land-owner—one of the proprietors of Portland in the early 1850s. Along with Thomas Dryer, he was responsible for publishing *The Weekly Oregonian*, the first Portland newspaper. He is remembered at Chapman School on NW Raleigh and at Chapman Square in SW Portland.

Left. *WPA artist Aimee Gorham created the splendid 1938 wood marquetry mural at Chapman Elementary School,* Send Us Forth to be Builders of a Better World.

NW RALEIGH STREET **TODAY**

Besaw's Restaurant (NW 21st), New Seasons Market Slabtown (NW 22nd), St. Jack (NW 23rd), Chapman School (NW 26th).

$\mathcal{S}$ IS FOR SAVIER

THOMAS A. SAVIER came to Portland in 1851 after digging for gold in the California dirt for a couple of years. His parents had come to Virginia from Italy, and were able to provide a first-rate education for their son Thomas. He had gone into the grain business with his brother before heading out west to seek his fortune. When he decided there was not enough gold in "them thar hills" he headed to Portland and returned to the grain market.

Savier worked in a general store on the waterfront before entering into a partnership with the owner. After the owner's death, he and Mr. Burnside got together to buy the business, paying the tidy sum of $120,000.[1]

First Choir of the First Congregational Church of Portland, Oregon; Thomas Savier, flute player, back row, second from left.[2]

56

Thomas Savier (1824-1876).[3]

He had found his gold in grain. Together they prospered and expanded into the international shipping business. Over the next 25 years Savier and his partner built a fleet of ships which sailed the seven seas.

Savier was rendered an invalid in his later years and journeyed to New York to seek treatment, but to no avail. Upon his death in 1876, he left behind his wife, a thriving company, and a street bearing his name.

Ordinance No. 7373

An Ordinance changing the name of Scott Street to Savier Street.

The City of Portland does Ordain as follows:

Section 1.— The Street in the City of Portland now Known and designated as Scott Street shall be Known and designated as Savier Street.

Approved, February 5th 1892.

W. S. Mason
Mayor

From 1/2/1892 to 2/5/1892 "S" Street was named Scott Street. This document, signed by Mayor William Spencer Mason, changes the name to Savier Street.[4] Snyder notes that Scott was one of the names under consideration for "S" Street.

NW SAVIER STREET **TODAY**

St. Patrick's Church (NW 19th), Forest Park Station U.S. Postal Service, (NW 24th).

$\mathcal{T}$ IS FOR THURMAN

IT SEEMS THAT there was some doubt over which Thurman was honored on this street. The 1921 *Oregonian* series on street names, after listing some of the Thurmans who had lived in Portland, concludes: "Men well informed in the history and the early citizenry of Portland are unable to recall the man for whom T Street was renamed and the doubt which now exists regarding the name of Thurman Street bids well to be permanent."[1]

This was not the first street where the identity of the person honored was clouded. Which Marshall, which Raleigh, and later which York were all in question. With all the attention that was given to this project, it is surprising that there was not a clearer record of the street namesakes.

As with all the other streets in Portland during the 1891 Great Street Renaming, Thurman received an entry that looked like this, as typed in the city log:[2]

> That "T" street in Willamette Heights Addition, Balch's Addition, Couch's Addition, Wilson's Addition, Murhard Tract and Watson's Addition all to the City of Portland be changed and hereafter known as Thurman street.

It was left to Snyder's comprehensive work on the subject in 1972 to give the nod to G. William Thurman (1855–1896). He based

The drinking fountain at NW 31st and Thurman was installed by Willamette Heights neighbors in 1916 to serve people, dogs, and horses. Today's neighbors celebrated its centennial in December 2016.

his conclusion on Thurman's contribution to Portland as an assistant manager of the Pacific Postal Telegraph Cable Company. Thurman was no doubt very good at his job but it was probably his friendship with Douglas Taylor that got him a street with his name on it. You will remember Mr. Taylor as the man in charge of naming the streets. Taylor was spared the temptation to name the street after himself. (SW Taylor Street in downtown Portland was already named, for President Zachary Taylor.[3])

Granville William Thurman resided at 545 ½ Washington Street. He died of Bright's disease, or kidney failure, at the age of 41.

In the more recent past, famed novelist and longtime Thurman Street resident Ursula K. Le Guin wrote *Blue Moon over Thurman Street* in 1994.

If you want to know more about the history of the street and not just the person, read this delightful book featuring Le Guin's jottings about the street where she lived, with accompanying photographs. We note with sadness her passing early in 2018 at the age of 88.

NW THURMAN STREET **TODAY**

Smith Teamaker (NW 17th), Cash and Carry (NW 19th), Multnomah County Library, Northwest Branch (NW 23rd), St. Honoré Bakery (NW 23rd Pl.), Food Front Coop (NW 23rd Pl.), Friendly House (NW 26th), Fat Tire Farm (NW 27th), Crackerjack's Pub & Eatery (NW 28th), the Balch Gulch Bridge (Thurman Street Viaduct) (NW 30th).

U IS FOR UPSHUR

ABEL PARKER UPSHUR (1790–1844) was a national figure and the only alphabet street namesake never to set foot in Portland. He was appointed secretary of the navy by President Tyler and in 1843 he succeeded Daniel Webster as secretary of state. A conservative Virginian, Upshur emerged as a leading pro-slavery advocate in the 1830s. In order to ward off Great Britain's interest in Texas, he pushed the United States toward annexation, calling it "the great object of my ambition". Although he did not live to see that annexation, his legacy is linked to the entry of Texas into the union as a slave state.[1]

He had no personal ties to the Oregon Territory. He did, however, actively promote the westward expansion of the United States. He

urged the extension of federal control over the Oregon Territory and he skillfully forged a compromise with Great Britain to make the 49th parallel the boundary with Canada. The Oregon Treaty of 1846 was completed under the following administration.

An unfortunate turn of events pre-

Abel Parker Upshur, Secretary vented Secretary of State Upshur from
of State (1843–44).[2]

AWFUL EXPLOSION of the "PEACE-MAKER" on board the U.S. STEAM FRIGATE, PRINCETON, on WEDNESDAY, 28th FEB! 1844

Explosion of the long gun the Peacemaker *on board the USS* Princeton, *1844.*[4]

welcoming Oregon into the Union as the 33rd state in 1859. In 1844 he was invited, along with President Tyler, to observe the firing of a cannon on the newly launched USS *Princeton*. One of the long guns, (mis)labeled the *Peacemaker*, and the second cannon, the *Oregon*, were at the time the navy's longest guns.[3]

While they were celebrating the occasion, the *Peacemaker* exploded, killing Upshur and several other dignitaries in attendance. The president was below deck at the time. For Upshur's efforts on behalf of the Oregon Territory, "U" Street was named in his honor, or perhaps because no other prominent pioneer names began with this unusual letter.

NW UPSHUR STREET **TODAY**

Globe Lighting Supply (NW 19th), Rae's Lakeview Lounge (NW 26th), Lower Macleay Park (NW 30th).

$\mathcal{V}$ IS FOR VAUGHN

SEVERAL POLITICIANS had their names given to Alphabet District streets, but only one Portland mayor—with the imposing name of George Washington Vaughn—received the honor. He was mayor only briefly (1855–56) and made his considerable wealth in various commercial enterprises.

Vaughn partnered with Captain Ankeny to run boats on the river, and he owned a hardware store and the first steam mill in Portland. Both buildings were destroyed in the Great Fire of 1873. The fire deserves a brief mention here, though it has been thoroughly documented in various histories, most recently in Dan Haneckow's excellent blog, *Café Unknown*.[1]

The Oregonian described the fire dramatically: "And lo! From the bosom of the city a slender spire of flames."[3] Vaughn's mill, worth $150,000, sustained the greatest damage and was insured for only $6,000.[4] The 1921 *Oregonian* article noted that the losses did not "leave him insolvent, and he was in good shape financially when he died on March 4, 1877."[5]

G.W. Vaughn (1813–1877).[2]

Vaughn Street Ballpark, early 1930s. (Courtesy of the Nelson Collection)

To the dwindling number of baseball lovers in Portland, Vaughn Street will always recall Vaughn Street Park, the original home of the Portland Beavers baseball team. It's where Slabtown's Johnny Pesky, Mr. Red Sox, honed his skills, and Satchel Paige, Ted Williams, and Mickey Lolich all made appearances.[6]

Two Northwest Portlanders who achieved national fame launched their careers at the ball park: Johnny Pesky (Paveskovich), an infielder for the Boston Red Sox in the '40s and '50s, and Mickey Lolich, an All-Star pitcher for the Detroit Tigers in the '60s and '70s. More recent heirs to the Vaughn Street Park legacy include two Portlanders, both Oregon Sports Hall of Famers: Pete Ward, who played third base for the Chicago White Sox, and Dale Murphy, a first baseman with the Atlanta Braves.

NW VAUGHN STREET TODAY

Esco Corporation (NW 25th) at the site of the old ball park, Meriwether's Restaurant (NW 26th), Montgomery Park (formerly Montgomery Ward) (NW 27th). (Vaughn Street changes its name at NW 27th to "Wardway" to honor Montgomery Ward and curves down to NW Industrial, leaving a new Vaughn Street to begin at NW 29th.)

$\mathcal{W}$IS FOR WILSON

DR. ROBERT B. WILSON is the second doctor honored by an alphabet street name. He preceded Dr. Glisan and is hailed by the historian Joseph Gaston as "the first physician of distinguished ability and education to settle and grow with the city."[1] Early on he alerted the city council to an outbreak of smallpox which led to some extraordinary measures aimed at containing it. One council motion required that "a flag twenty-one feet square shall float over each house in which the smallpox exists."[2]

Dr. Robert B. Wilson (1828–1887).[4] (Courtesy of OHSU)

He was a member of the original staff of Good Samaritan Hospital. His book collection (along with Dr. Glisan's) became the foundation of the original OHSU library, known as the R. B. Wilson Library from 1893 to 1919.[3]

He arrived in Portland, not unusually, after a gold-digging stint in California. But more unusually, he then became the ship doctor on the aptly named steamer, *Gold Hunter*, which carried goods and passengers between San Francisco and Portland. By

Willamette University Medical Department, a forerunner of OHSU, in 1889, NW 15th & "C" Street.[5] *The building was later used as the College of Dentistry and Pharmacy. (Courtesy of OHSU)*

late 1850 he decided not to return to the land of gold.

Instead, he remained here and married Captain Couch's eldest daughter Caroline, thus prompting the oft-quoted advice about how to get ahead in Portland ("join Trinity Church and marry a Couch"). He opened a practice upstairs at #5 Stark Street; his house was on North 4th Street (between B & C). During a lengthy illness in the last years of his life he left his office in the care of Dr. Glisan (who had also married a Couch daughter).

Dr. Wilson succumbed to pneumonia in 1887. He left behind seven children, two of whom became prominent Portland physicians.[6]

NW WILSON STREET **TODAY**

Clear Creek Distillery (NW 24th).

Y IS FOR YORK

NOTE: The street name is the same. The people honored are very different. Earlier writers had speculated that the street might have been named for the Rev. John York or a confectioner named Milton York. But the man we now honor was a slave known only as York.

As Portland prepared to commemorate the 2003–2006 bicentennial of the Lewis & Clark Expedition, the local planning group associated with the Oregon Historical Society (Lewis & Clark 2005) learned that the namesake of York Street was unknown. So it asked the city to declare that the "Y" Street be thereafter named for William Clark's slave, York.[1] Thus in 2002, the Portland City Council, with Mayor Vera Katz presiding, passed Resolution No. 36070 directing the Department of Transportation to record that the street honors York for "his role in the Lewis & Clark Expedition and the history of the City of Portland," making NW York Street the first street in the nation to do so.[2]

WHAT DO WE KNOW about Clark's slave York and how did he contribute to Portland's history? York (born in 1770) was a member of William Clark's small exploring party which canoed up the Willamette River and camped in the vicinity of today's St. John's Bridge in April 1806, thus making him the first black explorer to reach present-day Portland. By this time the historic expedition had already reached the Pacific Ocean, and York had become the first African-American to cross the continent north of Mexico.[3] These facts alone are enough to secure

York as depicted in an eight-story-high trompe l'oeil mural on the Oregon Historical Society's building, painted in 1989 by noted artist Richard Haas. The mural also depicts Lewis, Clark, Sacagawea, and the dog Seaman.

his place in Portland's history.

Much has been written about the curiosity with which Native Americans viewed York. They wanted to rub the paint off his skin, they attributed magical powers to him and called him "big medicine," and at times they were in awe of his strength and stature.

But York's contributions were far more than skin deep. Along the way and in all respects he proved himself a valuable member of the expedition. He carried a rifle, he hunted and scouted, and he was entrusted to trade on behalf of the expedition. When the Corps of Discovery, as it was known, reached the Pacific Ocean and built Fort Clatsop to spend the winter, York was consulted as an equal member of the group and his opinion was solicited along with the others. It was likely the first "vote" ever cast by an African-American slave.[4]

Yet, for all his skills and accomplishments, York remained a slave. And when the expedition returned to St. Louis in 1806 and others were rewarded with double pay and land grants, York continued to live in slavery. As Clark later wrote his brother: "I gave him a Severe trouncing the other Day but he has much mended Sence.[5] Clark finally freed him in 1816[6] but reported in 1832 that York had died of cholera many years earlier.

Portland filmmaker Ron Craig, in his award-winning documentary The Undiscovered Explorer: Imagining York, seeks to give voice to this heroic, yet tragic figure from our history, saying: "My goal is to take him where he couldn't go when he was alive."[7] York's name on "Y" Street is a small step in that direction.

The Forestry Building, an exhibition hall showcasing the timber industry at the 1905 Lewis & Clark Exposition, was said to be the largest log cabin in the world. It burned to the ground in a spectacular fire in 1964.

One hundred years after the Lewis & Clark Expedition, and abutting York Street in NW Portland, the 1905 Lewis & Clark Centennial Exposition marked the end of the old and the beginning of the new Oregon.[8] Portland closed the chapter on its pioneering days and heralded the birth of the city as we know it today. The Exposition lasted about five months and showcased exhibits from 21 countries and 16 states.[9] Most physical traces of the expedition have vanished but the economic impact was strong and lasting. Portland, in short, had entered the modern era and gained a worldwide audience.

And 200 years after the Lewis & Clark Expedition, a forward-looking Bicentennial group reached into the past and rededicated NW York Street in honor of a slave who had played such a significant role in the early explorations of Portland.

NW YORK STREET **TODAY**

A short street in industrial Northwest Portland. Bridgetown Coffee (NW 21st), Pearl Gallery and Fiction in the flex-use New York Building (NW 22nd).

POSTSCRIPT

WE HAVE COME TO THE END of the Great Street Renaming of 1891 but, of course, not quite to the end of the alphabet. Superintendent of Streets Taylor apparently could not find two worthy citizens whose names began with X and Z.

So instead, "X" Street eventually became Roosevelt and was so named in 1903 for President Theodore Roosevelt.[1] Roosevelt was the president at the time of the 1905 Lewis & Clark Exposition and he sent his vice president, Charles Fairbanks, to open the Exposition.[2] "Z" Street had already been named Reed Street in 1883 in honor of Simeon and Amanda Reed, later the benefactors of Reed College, and the name remained.[3]

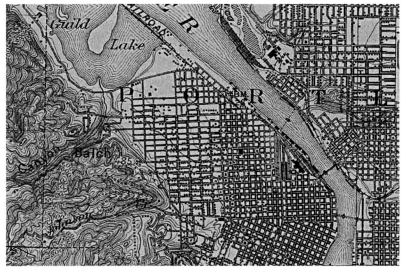

NW Portland in 1897, at the end of our story. Guild's Lake was still there, soon to host the 1905 Lewis & Clark Exposition. Union Station had by then replaced Couch Lake. Just before the Great Street Renaming of 1891, Albina and East Portland had merged with Portland into one city. Portland was ready for a new century.[4]

NOTES

INTRODUCTION

1. Carl Abbott, *Portland in Three Centuries: The Place and the People* (Corvallis: Oregon State University Press, 2011), 16. http://osupress.oregonstate.edu/sites/default/files/Abbott.PortlandinThreeCenturies.excerpt.pdf, accessed June 5, 2016.
2. Percy Maddux, *City on the Willamette* (Portland: Metropolitan Press, 1952), 24.
3. Richard Marlitt, *Nineteenth Street* (Portland: Oregon Historical Society, 1978).
4. E. Kimbark MacColl, *The Shaping of a City* (Portland: The Georgian Press Company, 1976), 5. (Frankfurt, Germany, and Hartford, Connecticut, were the first and second wealthiest cities in the world.)
5. Eugene Snyder, *Portland Names and Neighborhoods* (Portland: Binford & Mort, 1979), 53.
6. Snyder, *Portland Names*, 54.
7. Snyder, *Portland Names*, 55.
8. www.portlandoregon.gov/bps/article/149586.
9. www.portlandoregon.gov/bps/article/149586.
10. City of Portland Archives, Oregon, 7263 - Providing for the change of the names of Certain Streets in the City of Portland, Record Series 2001-07, 12/30/1891.
11. Jane Comerford, *A History of Northwest Portland: From the River to the Hills* (Portland, Dragonfly Press, 2011), 78.

A

1. The Southern Oregon Historical Society, "The Table Rock Sentinel," *The Ankeny Years*, in "Sunrise to Sunset at Sterlingville," March 1982, 11.
2. Portland's Skidmore Fountain, http://www.skidmoremarket.com/ under New Market Block, accessed May 2, 2016.
3. *The Ankeny Years*, 11.
4. Snyder, *Portland Names*, 88. Snyder gives an interesting and detailed accounting of the reasons for this narrow street called Ankeny.
5. http://www.saturdaymarket.com/, accessed May 2, 2016.

B

1. Snyder, *Portland Names*, 103.
2. Dan W. Burnside, ORG.Lot 108, "Notables" Collection, OHS.
3. Rebecca Koffman, "The Future of Old Chinatown," *The Oregonian*, March 11, 2014.
4. Snyder, *Portland Names*, 103.

C

1. Joseph Gaston, *The Centennial History of Oregon, 1811–1912, Vol. I* (Chicago: The S. J. Clarke Publishing Company, 1912), 373.
2. Joseph Gaston, *Portland, Its History and Builders, Vol. II* (Chicago: The S. J. Clarke Publishing Company, 1911), 375.
3. Snyder, *Portland Names*, 26.
4. Couch house photo, Oregon Historical Society, bb014237
5. William J. Hawkins III & William F. Willingham, *Classic Houses of Portland, Oregon* (Portland: Timber Press, 1999), 42.
6. National Park Service, Department of the Interior, "Balfour–Guthrie Building," Section 8, page 2, 8/1/02. The conversation actually took place in 1877 when the new manager of Balfour and Guthrie, Mr. Walter Burns, asked how to

succeed in Portland. http://focus.nps.gov/pdfhost/docs/NRHP/Text/02000824.
pdf, accessed June 6, 2016. *Note:* MacColl, *Shaping of a City*, n. 53 identifies
George Weidler as the one offering the advice. For additional evidence of
Couch as a 'founding father," MacColl calculates that besides his 4 daughters,
the Captain had "22 grandchildren, and 33 great-grandchildren." MacColl,
Shaping, n. 27.

7. Captain John Couch and his wife Caroline photo, Oregon Historical Society,
bb004081.
8. Snyder, *Portland Names*, 29.
9. "Sketches of Oregon," *The Morning Oregonian*, January 25, 1870, 1.
http://0-phw01.newsbank.com.catalog.multcolib.org/cache/ean/fullsize/
pl_006112016_1736_03114_41.pdf, accessed June 6, 2016.

D

1. Harvey Scott, *History of Portland, Oregon* (Syracuse: D. Mason and Company,
1890), 381.
2. E. Kimbark MacColl, *Merchants, Money, and Power: The Portland Establishment,
1843–1913* (Portland: Georgian Press, 1988), 110.
3. T. H. Crawford, *Historical Sketch of the Public Schools of Portland, Oregon,* 1847–1888,
4. http://www.pps.net/site/handlers/filedownload.ashx?moduleinstanceid=344&da-
taid=413&FileName=Historical-Sketch-PPS.pdf, accessed June 6, 2016.
4. Anthony L. Davis photo, Oregon Historical Society, bb015461.
5. Anthony L. Davis letter, March 1862, MSS1500, Preservation Copy, OHS.

E

1. *Wikipedia,* "Lovejoy Columns."
2. *The Morning Oregonian*, Everett, October 14, 1921, 12. http://0-phw02.
newsbank.com.catalog.multcolib.org/cache/ean/fullsize/pl_006112016 _2112
_30184_998.pdf, accessed June 10, 2016.
3. *The Evening Telegram,* August 23, 1902, Biography File, Oregon Historical Society.
4. *The Morning Oregonian*, Everett, October 14, 1921, 12.

F

1. Snyder, *Portland Names*, 130.
2. https://www.portlandoregon.gov/bps/article/146291, accessed May 21, 2016.
3. Captain George H. Flanders, MSS 1392, Oregon Historical Society.
4. Snyder, Eugene E., *Early Portland: Stump Town Triumphant 1831-1854* (Portland: Binford & Mort, 1970, 44-45).
5. Northwest District Association *Northwest Portland Historic Inventory, Historic
Context Statement, 1991,* 14. Along with Couch's brother-in-law Flanders, other
members of the Couch clan who moved to 19th Street included sons-in-law
Cicero Lewis and sons-in-law Dr. Rodney Glisan and Dr. Robert Wilson.
http://www.oregon.gov/oprd/HCD/OHC/docs/multnomah_portland_north-
west_historiccontext_vol1.pdf, accessed May 21, 2016. *Note:* Richard Marlitt,
Nineteenth Street (Portland: Oregon Historical Society, 1978). This book is a
revealing look at some of these mansions, inside and out. Much of the book is
dedicated to houses owned by the extended Couch family.
6. Flanders Mansion, c. 1870, ORHI 73272, Oregon Historical Society.
7. Joseph Gaston, *Portland: Its History and Builders Vol. I,* (Chicago–Portland: The
S. J. Clarke Publishing Co., 1911), 214. *Note:* Jewel Lansing, *Portland: People,
Politics, and Power 1851–2001* (Corvallis: Oregon State University Press, 2003),
139. Lansing contends that the East Side might very well have been the business hub of Portland had the fund drive for Union Station not been successful.

8. www.orhf.org/oregon-rail-heritage-center/our-locomotives/sp-4449/, accessed May 21, 2016.

9. "An Old Settler Dying," *The Sunday Oregonian*, November 20, 1892. http://0-infoweb.newsbank.com.catalog.multcolib.org/resources/doc/nb/image/, accessed May 21, 2016.

10. Gaston, *Portland: Its History and Builders Vol. II*, 522.

G

1. *Wikipedia*, "Rodney Glisan." https://en.wikipedia.org/wiki/Rodney_Glisan, accessed June 2, 2016.

2. Dr. Rodney Glisan (1827–1890). Olof Larsell Papers, OHSU Historical Collections & Archives, Portland, Oregon.

3. *Wikipedia*, "Rodney Glisan."

4. "Death of Dr. Rodney Glisan," *The Morning Oregonian*, June 4, 1890, 6, http://0-phw02.newsbank.com.catalog.multcolib.org/cache/ean/fullsize/pl_006112016_2137_43450_220.pdf, accessed June 2, 2016.

5. *Wikipedia*, "Rodney Glisan."

6. Certificate photo courtesy of Multnomah County Library. Multnomah County Library Membership for Dr. Rodney Glisan, https://gallery.multcolib.org/image/certificate-perpetual-membership-no-4-dr-rodney-glisan, accessed June 2, 2016.

H

1. James D. Miller, "Early Oregon Scenes: A Pioneer Narrative, Vol. II," in *Oregon Historical Quarterly* 31, no. 2 (June, 1930), 160–180. Portland: Oregon Historical Society, http://www.jstor.org/stable/20610551, accessed June 5, 2016.

2. Snyder, *Portland Names*, 131.

3. *Wikipedia*, poet signed "O.P.Q." in *Oregon Spectator*, August 19, 1851. As quoted in Mills, *Sternwheelers up Columbia* (Pacific Books, 1947), 22. https://en.wikipedia.org/wiki/Multnomah_%28sidewheeler_1851%29, accessed June 8, 2016.

4. *Wikipedia*, "Steamboats of the Columbia River." Date and location of photograph established from Wright, ed., Lewis and Dryden Marine History, 34. https://en.wikipedia.org/wiki/Multnomah_%28sidewheeler_1851%29, accessed June 8, 2016.

5. Lone Fir Cemetery Grave Marker. http://www.findagrave.com/cgi-bin/fg.cgi?page=gr&GRid=59319741, accessed May 24, 2016.

I

1. *Wikipedia*, "Steamboats of the Columbia River," https://en.wikipedia.org/wiki/Steamboats_of_the_Columbia_River, accessed May 15, 2016.

2. *Wikipedia*, "William Irving (Steamship Captain)," https://en.wikipedia.org/wiki/William_Irving_%28steamship_captain%29, accessed May 17, 2016.

3. Snyder, *Portland Names*, 155.

4. *Wikipedia*, "Couch Family Investment Development," https://en.wikipedia.org/wiki/File:Couch_Family_Investment_Development_no3_-_Portland_Oregon.jpg, accessed May 17, 2016.

J

1. Snyder, *Portland Names*, 157. *Note:* See Mike Ryerson, Norm Gholston, and Tracy J. Prince, *Portland's Slabtown* (Charleston: Arcadia Publishing, 2013) for more history and photographs of these creeks.

2. Scott, *History of Portland*, 563.

3. Classified Ad, *The Morning Oregonian*, August 26, 1876.

4. The Johnson Estate, c. 1865, Neg. No. 38232-a, Oregon Historical Society.
5. The City of Portland, "King's Hill Historic District Guidelines," 116. https://www.portlandoregon.gov/bps/article/58856, accessed May 26, 2016.
6. The City of Portland, "Kings Hill," 111. https://www.portlandoregon.gov/bps/article/58856, accessed May 26, 2016.

K

1. http://www.usmarshals.gov/readingroom/us_marshals/oregon.pdf, accessed June 4, 2016. http://www.historylink.org/index.cfm?DisplayPage=output.cfm&file_id=essay 5238, accessed June 4, 2016.
2. Snyder, *Portland Names*, 158.
3. *The Morning Oregonian*, October 19, 1921, 13. http://0-phw02.newsbank.com.catalog.multcolib.org/cache/ean/fullsize/pl_006112016_1739_45726_526.pdf, accessed June 4, 2016
4. *The Morning Oregonian*, October 19, 1921, 13.
5. *Encyclopedia of Washington State History*, "McNeil Island and the Federal Penitentiary, 1841–1981." http://www.historylink.org/index.cfm?DisplayPage=output.cfm&file_id=5238, accessed June 8, 2016.

PORTLAND & "THE SIMPSONS" CONNECTION

1. Scott Cook and Aimee Wade, *PDXccentric—The Odyssey of Portland Oddities* (Slough Biscuit Press, 2014), 93.
2. "Top 10 Best Ned Flanders Quotes," #5, #2, http://www.top10-best.com/n/top_10_best_ned_flanders_quotes.html, accessed April 7, 2016.
3. http://simpsons.wikia.com/wiki/Kearney_Zzyzwicz, accessed April 7, 2016.
4. https://escapetoreality.org/2010/04/01/christianity-in-the-simpsons-top-12-reverend-lovejoy-quotes/, accessed April 7, 2016.
5. "The Eighteenth Amendment, Quotes," http://simpsons.wikia.com/wiki/Homer_vs._the_Eighteenth_Amendment/Quotes, accessed April 8, 2016.

L

1. Asa Lovejoy photo, Oregon Historical Society, #bb000666.
2. The coin is now displayed in the lobby of the Oregon Historical Society. The passing years have spawned numerous versions of this famous coin toss. The most comprehensive collection of these tales can be found at the informative Dan Haneckow blog, *Café Unknown.com*, under the heading "The Vexed Question." In a much earlier article in the *Oregon Native Son* magazine, "Portland Oregon, Its Founders and Early Businessmen," the writer is quoted as saying that this Matron Head penny was "no doubt then the only one in Oregon." *The Oregon Native Son*, Vol. II, 1901, 331. https://books.google.com/books?id=N8AUAAAAYAAJ&dq=The+Oregon+native+son+1901&source=gbs_navlinks_s, accessed June 7, 2016.

M

1. Snyder, *Portland Names*, 176. As quoted in Marshall, *The Morning Oregonian*, October 26, 1921, 13. http://0-phw02.newsbank.com.catalog.multcolib.org/cache/ean/fullsize/pl_006112016_1744_23925_800.pdf, accessed May 22, 2016.
2. *The Oregonian* July 30, 1962, 10, accessed June 10, 2016.
3. John Marshall, *Lewis & Dryden's Marine History of the Pacific Northwest*, 57.
4. *The Morning Oregonian* August 23, 1921, 20. http://0-phw01.newsbank.com.catalog.multcolib.org/cache/ean/fullsize/pl_006112016_2102_39800_459.pdf, accessed June 5, 2016.
5. Gaston, *Portland, Oregon*, Vol. II, 776.

6. *The Morning Oregonian*, August 23, 1921.

N

1. Edward J. Northrup, rootsweb.ancestry.com, http://www.rootsweb.ancestry.com/~ormultno/History/Scott/biogM-S/northrup.htm, accessed May 2, 2016.
2. *Oregon Native Son*, Vol. II, "Edward J. Northrup," May 1900, 45.
3. *The Morning Oregonian*, July 25, 1878 2. http://0-infoweb.newsbank.com.catalog.multcolib.org/resources/doc/nb/image/v2%3A11A73E582761 8330%40EANX-NB-12349AC92F7FBAA0%402407191-122FAC-25733C3218%401-12D4BB65C2E8A100%40No%2BHeadline?p=AMNEWS, accessed June 5, 2016.
4. Northrup House, Oregon Historical Society, order # 021708.
5. Edward J. Northrup photo, http://www.findagrave.com/cgi-bin/fg.cgi?page=pv&GRid=52226550&PIpi=90259423, accessed June 8, 2016.
6. Scott, *History of Portland*, 624.
7. U.S. Department of the Interior, "National Register of Historic Places Inventory,"
8. http://focus.nps.gov/GetAsset?assetID=09b33739-87db-4916-bf3b-dd55 fe603294, accessed June 8, 2016.

O

1. Senator J. W. Nesmith, "Oregon Pioneer Association Transactions for 1875," 57. https://archive.org/stream/OregonPioneerAssociationTransactions-For1875/75-OPA-Transactions-03_djvu.txt, accessed April 4, 2016.
2. Scott, *History of Portland*, 81
3. "One History Sleuth's Radical Theory: Everything We Know About How Portland Began Is Wrong," *Portland Monthly*, Leah Sottile, May 19, 2016. http://www.pdxmonthly.com/articles/2016/5/19/one-history-sleuth-s-radical-theory-everything-we-know-about-how-portland-began-is-wrong, accessed July 9, 2016.
4. Overton's signature, Oregon State Archives, courtesy of Randall Trowbridge.
5. Portland 1851, Oregon Historical Society, bb014236
6. T. T. Geer, *Fifty Years in Oregon* (New York, The Neale Publishing Co., 1912). Chapter XIX, Diary entry February 24, 1848. http://www.theragens.com/fifty_years/fifty_years_in_oregon_18-19.htm, accessed April 4, 2016.

P

1. Francis Pettygrove photo, Oregon Historical Society, bb002972.
2. MacColl, *Merchants, Money and Power*, 10.
3. *The Morning Oregonian*, May 23, 1915, accessed 01/25/2018.
4. *The Morning Oregonian*, April 17, 1916, accessed 01/25/2018.
5. MacColl, *Merchants, Money and Power*, 11.
6. Daniel Lownsdale deserves mention here in the story of early Portland even though his name is not on an alphabet street. It has been noted that his tannery was a great boon to the development of commerce in early Portland. Tanner Creek, on which he built his business, runs (now underground) through Northwest Portland. His contribution is celebrated at Tanner Springs Park, NW 10th Avenue and Marshall, just before the creek empties into the Willamette River.

Q

1. *Portrait and Biographical Record of the Willamette Valley, Oregon* (Chicago, Chapman Publishing Co., 1903), 185.
2. U.S. Department of the Interior, Skidmore/Old Town Historic District, 47,

https://www.nps.gov/nhl/apply/pdfs/Criterion5_Skidmore.pdf, accessed May 27, 2016. *Note:* In 1873, Portland had one liquor outlet for every 205 people. By loose comparison, LaCrosse, Wisconsin, which has more bars per person than any other US city today, has only 0.14 bars for every 205 people. http://247wallst.com/special-report/2016/05/14/the-drunkest-and-driest-cities-in-america/4/, accessed June 5, 2016.

3. *The Morning Oregonian*, April 26, 1907, 9.
4. Louise Swan, "Perkins decided to build a new hotel," as quoted in *Northwest Magazine*, May 3, 1981, 7. https://vintageportland.files.wordpress.com/2011/04/perkins-hotel-19810503a.pdf, accessed June 5, 2016.
5. http://www.wweek.com/portland/article-10491-stamps-of-approval.html, accessed June 5, 2016.
6. *The Morning Oregonian*, October 24, 1921, 6. http://0-phw02.newsbank.com.catalog.multcolib.org/cache/ean/fullsize/pl_006112016_2024_59154_265.pdf, accessed June 5, 2016.
7. Portland Archives and Record Center (PARC), 1886 Directory, Box Number 2616, A2012-030.

R

1. Snyder, *Portland Names*, 193.
2. Oregon Blue Book, "List of Employees in Custom Service, Port of Portland, Oregon, District of Willamette," 185. https://books.google.com/books?id=LD00AQAAMAAJ&dq=A.E.+raleigh+portland&source=gbs_navlinks_s, accessed April 2, 2016.
3. *The Morning Oregonian*, November 19, 1895, 5. http://0-phw02.newsbank.com.catalog.multcolib.org/cache/ean/fullsize/pl_006112016_1840_25549_216.pdf, accessed May 25, 2016.
4. *The Morning Oregonian*, November 25, 1897, accessed 01/22/18.

S

1. Gaston, History of Portland, Vol. II, 593.
2. City of Portland Archives, Oregon, A2004-002.
3. Thomas A. Savier, 1824-1876, OHS, Notables Collection, ORG LOT 108.
4. City of Portland Archives, Oregon, 7373 Changing the Name of Scott St. to Savier St., Record Series 2001-07, 02/05/1892.

T

1. *The Morning Oregonian*, October 28, 1921, 13. http://0-phw01.newsbank.com.catalog.multcolib.org/cache/ean/fullsize/pl_006112016_2031_03572_737.pdf, accessed June 5, 2016.
2. City of Portland Archives, Oregon, 7263 – Providing for the change of the names of Certain Streets in the City of Portland, Record Series 2001-07, 12/30/1891.
3. Snyder, *Portland Names*, 213.

U

1. Snyder, *Portland Names*, 221.
2. *Wikipedia*, Portrait by A. G. Heaton, https://en.wikipedia.org/wiki/Abel_P._Upshur, accessed June 5, 2016.
3. Ann Blackman, "Fatal Cruise of the Princeton" in *Navy History*, September, 2005. http://www.military.com/NewContent/0,13190,NH_0905_Cruise-P1,00.html, accessed May 29, 2016.

4. *Wikipedia*, "The USS Princeton disaster of 1844." https://en.wikipedia.org/wiki/USS_Princeton_disaster_of_1844#/media/File:Explosion_aboard_USS_Princeton.jpg, N. Currier (firm) – Library of Congress, Prints & Photographs Division, LC-USZC2-3201 (color film copy slide), archival TIFF version (4 MB), accessed June 5, 2016.

V

1. Dan Haneckow, *Café Unknown*. http://www.cafeunknown.com/2007/11/city-in-flames-london-chicago-san.html, accessed April 20, 2016. The blog is full of history and photographs of this major fire.
2. George W. Vaughn, Oregon Historical Society, Notables Collection, ORG LOT 108.
3. *The Morning Oregonian*, August 4, 1873, http://0-phw02.newsbank.com.catalog.multcolib.org/cache/ean/fullsize/pl_006112016_1844_27571_977.pdf, accessed June 5, 2016.
4. MacColl, *Merchants, Money, and Power*, 175.
5. *The Morning Oregonian*, October 29, 1921, 12. http://0-phw01.newsbank.com.catalog.multcolib.org/cache/ean/fullsize/pl_006112016_2041_29226_536.pdf, accessed June 9, 2016.
6. PdxHistory.com, "Portland Baseball." http://www.pdxhistory.com/html/portland_baseball.html, accessed June 5, 2016.

W

1. Gaston, *Portland, Its History and Builders, Vol. III*, 16.
2. Lansing, *Portland*, 61.
3. "History of the OHSU Library," http://www.ohsu.edu/xd/education/library/about/collections/historical-collections-archives/about/histoflibshort.cfm, accessed June 5, 2016.
4. Dr. R. B. Wilson (1828–1887). Olof Larsell Papers, OHSU Historical Collections & Archives, Portland, Oregon.
5. Willamette Medical Department, 15th and Couch Street, erected 1889. Olof Larsell Papers, OHSU Historical Collections & Archives, Portland, Oregon.
6. *Oregon Native Son*, Vol I, 404.

Y

1. *The Skanner*, May 22, 2002, Portland, Oregon, Volume XXVII, No. 34.
2. City of Portland, Vera Katz, Mayor, Resolution 36070, May 22, 2002.
3. Fred Leeson, "Portland Street now named for black explorer" in *The Oregonian*, May 23, 2002. http://0-infoweb.newsbank.com.catalog.multcolib.org/resources/doc/nb/news/0F3BA0A343F2ABEF?p=AMNEWS, accessed October 29, 2016.
4. Robert B. Betts, *In Search of York* (University Press of Colorado, 1985), p. 41.
5. Steve Beaven, *The Oregonian*, May 8, 2010. http://www.oregonlive.com/news/index.ssf/2010/05/statue_at_lewis_clark_college.html, accessed October 29, 2016.
6. Fred Leeson, *The Oregonian*, May 23, 2002.
7. Fred Leeson, *The Oregonian*, May 23, 2002.
8. Carl Abbott, *The Great Extravaganza*, Portland and the Lewis and Clark Exposition, (Portland: Oregon Historical Society, 2004), 59.
9. *Wikipedia* "Lewis and Clark Centennial Exposition and Records Center." https://en.wikipedia.org/wiki/Lewis_and_Clark_Centennial_Exposition, accessed June 5, 2016.

POSTSCRIPT

1. "Alphabet District Street Names," http://www.portlandhometeam.com/alphabet-district-street-names.php, accessed June 5, 2016.
2. Carl Abbott, *The Great Extravaganza*, 3 (facing).
3. Facts About Reed, "Mission and History," https://www.reed.edu/about_reed/history.html, accessed June 5, 2016.
4. 1897 Map of Portland, https://www.lib.utexas.edu/maps/historical/portland_or_1897.jpg, accessed June 5, 2016.

BIBLIOGRAPHY

Abbott, Carl. *The Great Extravaganza, Portland and the Lewis and Clark Exposition*, Portland: Oregon Historical Society, 2004

Betts, Robert B., *In Search of York*. University Press of Colorado and the Lewis and Clark Trail Heritage Foundation, 1985.

Blalock, Barney. *Portland's Lost Waterfront*. Charleston: The History Press, 2012.

Comerford, Jane. *A History of Northwest Portland: From the River to the Hills*. Portland: Dragonfly Press, 2011.

Gaston, Joseph. *Portland, Its History and Builders, Vols. I, II, III*. Chicago: The S. J. Clarke Publishing Company, 1911.

Geer, T.T. *Fifty Years in Oregon*. New York: The Neale Publishing Co., 1912.

Gorseck, Christopher S. *Portland's Pearl District*. Charleston: Arcadia Publishing, 2012.

Harrison, Rebecca and Daniel Cowan. *Portland's Maritime History*. Charleston: Arcadia Publishing, 2014.

Hawkins, William John III. *The Grand Era of Cast Iron Architecture in Portland*. Portland: Binford & Mort Publishers, 1976.

Hawkins, William J. III and William F. Willingham. *Classic Houses of Portland, Oregon 1850–1950*. Portland: Timber Press, Inc., 2005.

Lansing, Jewel. *Portland People, Politics, and Power 1851–2001*. Corvallis, Oregon: Oregon State University Press, 2005.

Larsell, Olof. *The Doctor in Oregon*. Portland: Binfords & Mort for the Oregon Historical Society, 1947.

MacColl, E. Kimbark. *Merchants, Money and Power*. Portland: The Georgian Press Company, 1988.

MacColl, E. Kimbark. *The Shaping of a City*. Portland: The Georgian Press Company, 1976.

Maddux, Percy. *City on the Willamette*. Portland: Metropolitan Press, 1952.

Marschner, Janice. Oregon 1859, *A Snapshot in Time*. Portland: Timber Press, 2009.

Marlitt, Richard. *Nineteenth Street*. Portland: Oregon Historical Society, 1978.

Ryerson, Mike, Norm Gholston, and Tracy J. Prince. *Portland's Stabtown*. Charleston: Arcadia Publishing, 2013.

Scott, Harvey. *History of Portland, Oregon*. Syracuse: D. Mason & Co., 1890.

Snyder, Eugene E. *Early Portland: Stump-Town Triumphant 1831–1854*. Portland: Binford & Mort, 1970.

Snyder, Eugene E. *Portland Names and Neighborhoods: Their Historic Origins*. Portland, Binford & Mort, 1979.

OTHER RESOURCES

Dan Haneckow, *Café Unknown*, blog
Randall Trowbridge, interview
findagrave.com (online)
Multnomah County Library
Portland Archives and Records Center (PARC)
OHSU Historical Collections and Archives
Oregon Historical Society

Portland Monthly
Portland Tribune
The Morning Oregonian (online)
The NW Examiner
The Oregonian (online)
Wikipedia (online)